PENGUIN BOOK

SATYAJIT RAY IN 100 ANECDOTES

Arthy Muthanna Singh is a children's writer, freelance journalist, copywriter, editor and cartoonist based in Gurugram. She grew up on tea plantations in the Nilgiris. She has authored over thirty books for children and has been helping her mother conduct the Ooty Literary Festival since 2016. She was with *Limca Book of Records* for about thirteen years. She hopes to settle down in Coonoor or Goa someday soon.

Mamta Nainy is a children's writer and editor based in New Delhi. She spent some years in advertising before an apple fell on her head while she was sitting under a mango tree and she had her Eureka moment. She has been writing for children since then. She has authored many books for children, including *A Brush with Indian Art* which won The Hindu Young World-Goodbooks Award 2019 for Best Book (Non-Fiction).

PENGUIN BOOKS

USA | Canada | UK | Ireland | Australia
New Zealand | India | South Africa | China

Penguin Books is part of the Penguin Random House group of companies
whose addresses can be found at global.penguinrandomhouse.com

Published by Penguin Random House India Pvt. Ltd
7th Floor, Infinity Tower C, DLF Cyber City,
Gurgaon 122 002, Haryana, India

First published in Penguin Books by Penguin Random House India 2021

ISBN 9780143453048

Layout and Design by Aniruddha Mukherjee
Typeset in Droid Serif by Syllables27, New Delhi
Printed at Replika Press Pvt. Ltd, India

www.penguin.co.in

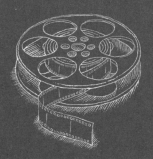

SATYAJIT RAY IN
100
ANECDOTES

WRITTEN BY ARTHY MUTHANNA SINGH AND MAMTA NAINY

ILLUSTRATIONS BY ANIRUDDHA MUKHERJEE AND CHARULATA MUKHERJEE

INTRODUCTION BY DHRITIMAN CHATERJI

PENGUIN BOOKS

An imprint of Penguin Random House

Read Books by Satyajit Ray

The Adventures of Feluda: The Golden Fortress

The Adventures of Feluda: The Secret of the Cemetery

The Adventures of Feluda: The Mystery of the Elephant God

The Adventures of Feluda: The Royal Bengal Mystery

The Adventures of Feluda: Trouble in Gangtok

The Adventures of Feluda: The Bandits of Bombay

The Adventures of Feluda: The Curse of the Goddess

The Adventures of Feluda: The Criminals of Kathmandu

The Adventures of Feluda: The House of Death

The Adventures of Feluda: The Emperor's Ring

The Puffin Feluda Omnibus: Volume 1

On the Run with Fotikchand (Classic Adventures)

The Exploits of Professor Shonku: The Unicorn Expedition and Other Stories

Puffin Classics: The Diary of a Space Traveller and Other Stories

Puffin Classics: The Mystery of Munroe Island and Other Stories

Puffin Classics: The Final Adventures of Professor Shonku

Puffin Classics: One Dozen Stories

Puffin Classics: Another Dozen Stories

INTRODUCTION

Once upon a time long ago, we lived in a quiet little lane in South Calcutta. Just opposite was the small, unpretentious studio where Satyajit Ray edited his films. Our son was a lively five at the time and ran all over the place, with nearly all the neighbours keeping an eye on him.

Then one evening, he couldn't be found. Frantic searches were mounted in the alleys and the homes he went to. No sign. To say that we were all getting a bit panicky would be understating it. Suddenly, we heard a very relieved yell: 'There's Pablo.' Everybody crowded around the door of the smallish room where Ray used to work. There he sat at the Moviola editing machine, intently explaining something to Pablo who was nestled in his lap. Both seemed quite oblivious to the fuss going on all around.

Right from *Pather Panchali*, through *Pikoor Diary* and on to the Feluda films, Ray seemed to have a special bond with children, the ability to communicate with them and treat them as people who needed to be talked to seriously. When he wrote for children, he did so to entertain and to educate but without talking down to them. And what he wrote for children could be enjoyed by adults as well. I discovered this when diving deep into the Professor Shonku stories to prepare to play the eccentric scientist in a film.

It is so very appropriate, then, that his birth centenary should be commemorated with a book that brings 100 incidents and anecdotes from his rich and varied life to readers in crisp, lively, finely illustrated accounts. On the face of it, the anecdotes may appear random but, taken together, they provide a kind of overview to the life of a fascinating man.

Arthy Muthanna Singh and Mamta Nainy have been producing entertaining and educative literature for children for the past two years, including a book on the Mahatma in 150 episodes. Their hard work for the current book is evident. They have dug out seemingly innocuous but unusual nuggets of information from various sources.

Get ready to be surprised!

Dhritiman Chaterji
February 2021
Goa

PREFACE

One of the things about artists and writers you've grown up admiring and whose creative worlds you've inhabited in your head for far too long is that you feel like you've *known* them forever; that in some parallel universe you're connected with them because you've taken something from their art and stories and language and, in that process, they've become one of your own. This holds truer than true for Manik Da—the towering figure of Indian cinema and literature, the great Satyajit Ray.

A master film-maker, a remarkable auteur, a writer par excellence and an artist of immense reach and range, Ray flitted from form to form with boundless ease and his diverse talent coalesced to produce works that could be distinguished by a rare sympathy and compassion, a deep humanism that finds resonance with people across generations, aesthetic tastes and interests. And, like Tagore before him, Ray will always appeal to those whose sensitivities allow them to probe deeper into human beings and the human condition. But despite being one of India's most composite artists, someone whose films, books and thinking have permeated into the existence of cinema connoisseurs, art aficionados and literature lovers for many decades, there has always been an enigma of sorts around the man that Satyajit Ray was. During the birth centenary of Ray (1921–2021), would it not be worthwhile to revisit his life and works that made our world so very luminous? In this question lay the beginnings of this book—a book that's a special blend of biography and lore, and every page of which is an engaging and illuminating yarn from the life story of Ray.

We must confess though that we had never been more exhilarated and frightened before any project as we were when we started working on this book. It was *the* Satyajit Ray that we'd be writing about, after all. To say that the task was daunting would be an understatement. But, as we started revisiting his life and times and rereading his works, the joys we garnered from them were so vast and diverse that every fear went out the window. That Manik Da was a genius we never doubted, but after trying to get a perspective of the man as regards his life and work, his interests and passions, his inspirations and reflections, the admiration only grew.

And now that the book is in your hands, dear reader, we only hope that the joys we derived from writing this book find their way to you as well . . .

Arthy Muthanna Singh and Mamta Nainy
February 2021
Gurugram and Delhi

'The only solutions that are ever worth anything
are the solutions that people find themselves.'

—Satyajit Ray

1

An Artist is Born

Satyajit Ray was born on 2 May 1921 into one of the most remarkable families of nineteenth-century Calcutta (now Kolkata)—the Rays. From printing technology to religious reforms, from painting to children's literature, from music and science to education of women, the Ray family was at the leading edge of a range of sociocultural reforms at the time. Satyajit Ray's grandfather, Upendrakishore Ray Chowdhury, was a painter, writer, violinist and an amateur astronomer. He was closely associated with India's social reformist Brahmo Samaj movement. Ray's father, Sukumar Ray, was one of the most original and captivating writers for children. And his mother, Suprabha Devi, was a proficient singer. Many of his relatives were accomplished scientists, photographers, artists and physicians.

Without a Father

2

Sukumar Ray was one of India's first writers of nonsense literature. His indigenous characters and allusions have been intrinsic to children in Bengali families across generations. Sadly, he fell ill soon after Satyajit Ray was born. When Satyajit Ray was just two years old, his father died of kala-azar or black fever at only thirty-five. Ray never had a chance to get to know his father. It was only much later that he could grasp who his father had been through his writing, art and what his mother and other relatives told him.

3

The Sighting of a Ship

Satyajit Ray had very few memories of his father. One incident that Ray clearly remembered about his father, though, was from a time when they had gone to Sodepur, a small town in the northern suburbs of Calcutta, for the sake of his father's health. The house they stayed in was by the Ganga and had a small courtyard. One day, his father was sitting by the window and painting. Satyajit heard him exclaim loudly, 'Look, a ship!' When Satyajit ran out into the courtyard, he saw a steamer pass by—his first sighting of a ship.

Finding Water

When Sukumar Ray was ailing, the family went to Giridih (now in Jharkhand) for a change of air. One evening, little Satyajit—or Manik as he was lovingly called—and their long-time house help Prayag were sitting on the banks of River Usri. Prayag told him that if he dug the sand deep enough, he would find water. With his wooden toy spade, Manik started to dig the sand excitedly. Soon enough, water started trickling out of the sand. Just then, a little girl from the nearby village came and started washing her hands in the water. Manik was visibly annoyed. 'How can she wash her hands in the water that I've found!' he said, irritated.

5

U Ray and Sons

Ray was born in his ancestral mansion in Calcutta—100 A, Garpar Road, and lived there until he was five. Designed by his grandfather Upendrakishore Ray Chowdhury, the mansion also housed a printing press. On the front wall of the mansion was written 'U RAY AND SONS, PRINTERS AND BLOCK MAKERS'* in big letters. Upendrakishore also founded the much-beloved Bengali children's magazine *Sandesh* and printed it in his printing press. After Upendrakishore's death, Sukumar Ray took over the job of editing and printing the magazine. Satyajit Ray's early years were spent in an environment of halftone blocks, cameras and darkrooms. He would visit the press in the afternoons to find type compositors sitting in rows, bent over their multi-compartmented type cases. They picked out letters and arranged them carefully to match the text—something that fascinated little Satyajit no end.

This house has been declared a heritage building by the Kolkata Municipal Corporation.

The Paint Box

Upendrakishore Ray Chowdhury died five-and-a-half years before Satyajit Ray was born. On the second floor of their Garpar residence was Upendrakishore's study, which remained empty after his death. One day, Satyajit went to the study and found a wooden box in which his grandfather kept his paints, brushes and bottles of linseed oil. He was very excited to find this box. He used up all its contents to create drawings and paintings on many a lazy afternoon.

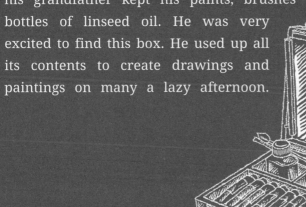

7

A Mother's Influence

Being from a family of creative and literary stalwarts like Upendrakishore Ray Chowdhury and Sukumar Ray, it is easy to forget that Ray's mother Suprabha was the one who brought him up almost single-handedly. Soon after Satyajit was born, Sukumar Ray fell ill and subsequently died. From the age of two years and four months, Satyajit was raised by Suprabha alone. It must have been so difficult for her to cope as a widow so early in life, while looking after a young son. She was his teacher until he started attending a formal school. She would read out stories by Arthur Conan Doyle to him in English and then translate them into Bengali—to make it easier for the young boy to understand. Every year, she would take Ray to Whiteaway Laidlaw & Co.—one of the poshest department stores in Calcutta during the British rule in India—to buy him crackers for Kali Puja. Ray and his mother shared a very special bond!

A Woman of Many Talents

Suprabha Ray even took up a job, which was uncommon in those days. She travelled by bus every day to Vidyasagar Bani Bhawan (Widows' Home) to teach the women to sew and embroider, something she was very skilled at. She was brilliant at Kashmiri embroidery. In fact, the Kashmiri *kadhaiwallahs*, people who used to come to Calcutta from Kashmir to sell their embroidered fabrics, would be stunned at her beautiful embroidery. Suprabha Devi was a brilliant cook and excelled at making both vegetarian and non-vegetarian dishes. She was a good singer too—she had even recorded a song with HMV in Calcutta. Sculpting was another talent that she possessed. She had sculpted a lovely bust of Gautama Buddha, which later occupied a pride of place in Satyajit Ray's home.

The Selection of Samples

After his father's death, Satyajit's uncle, Subinoy Ray, took charge of the printing press. He would order paper samples of varied kinds—thick and thin, glazed and matte, coarse and smooth—from Germany. Sometimes, when little Satyajit visited his room, his uncle would promptly hand the book of paper samples to him and ask him to choose the ones he should order. Satyajit would take his time, running his hand over each and every sample and feeling its surface. After much deliberation, as if he were an expert, he would tell his uncle the ones that he'd liked—mighty convinced that these were the exact ones that his uncle would order from Germany!

The Little Artist

One of the first childhood wonders that Satyajit encountered was a process camera that stood in the middle of their printing press. It was operated by a man named Ramdaheen. Sometimes, when Ray visited the printing press, he would pick up a piece of paper and doodle a funny portrait or a cartoon on it and pass it to Ramdaheen. 'This must come out in the next issue of *Sandesh*,' Satyajit would tell Ramdaheen, who would nod vigorously and say, 'Of course, Khokababu!' Ramdaheen would place his drawing under the lens of the camera to show him the inverted image of it through the glass behind the camera as little Satyajit stared at the upside-down image in great amazement.

11

The Uncle with Zany Habits

Many people apart from Satyajit and his mother lived in the house-cum-press, U Ray and Sons at 100 A, Garpar Road. Among them were Ray's grandmother, his uncles—Sukumar Ray's younger brothers—and even his grandfather's brother. The one thing that Satyajit Ray remembered very clearly about his younger uncle Subimal Ray, or Chotto Kaka as he called him, was how he spent at least an hour more than the others to finish his meals. This was because he believed that each mouthful had to be chewed exactly thirty-two times for food to get properly digested!

The House with a Zoo

Satyajit Ray's father and grandfather had many illustrious friends. One of them was Sir Jagadish Chandra Bose. A great scientist, he studied plant physiology and proved that plants have life. He was honoured with a knighthood for his work. Sir Jagadish Chandra Bose lived on Upper Circular Road, which was quite close to the Ray residence on Garpar Road. Ray, as a child, often visited his house and always looked forward to the visits. The reason, however, was not to meet the world-renowned scientist but to see the small zoo that Jagadish Chandra Bose had next to the garden in his home, which housed all kinds of animals!

13

The First Friend

Ray had no siblings. But that did not leave him in want of company. One of the first friends he made was the son of their housemaid Shyama, Chhedi. Chhedi was five years older than him and always called him Ray Chowdhury. He was a skilled kite-flyer. The festival of Vishwakarma Puja—when machines are worshipped for their smooth functioning and virtually everyone in Calcutta engages in kite-flying competitions—was especially exciting for Satyajit. Early in the morning on the day of the puja, Chhedi scrambled his way to the rooftop, Satyajit in tow, and exhibited his skills in kite-flying battles. Satyajit held the reel as Chhedi's kite wandered the skies. Each time Chhedi cut an opponent's kite and captured it, the sky echoed with jubilant cries from neighbourhood houses—*Bhokatta*! Your kite is gone!

An Unusual Lantern

Chhedi was not just good at flying kites but also at making a variety of unusual things that piqued young Satyajit's curiosity and were a source of constant joy for him. One of these extraordinary things that Chhedi made was a lamp from an empty clay pot of yoghurt. Chhedi would take an earthen pot, remove its circular bottom and cover it with a piece of coloured glass. He would place a candle inside it and cover the mouth of the pot with a cardboard lid. He would pierce a hole on the cardboard lid to let the air in so that the flame wouldn't go out. Finally, he tied a string around the neck of the pot and carried it around. A soft, coloured light emanated from this pot-lantern—a lantern the likes of which Satyajit had never seen before or after!

15

A Chair or Weighing Machine

When Ray was a child, all the big shops and fancy stores in Calcutta were in Chowringhee. But there was one shop called Carr and Mahalanobis in Whiteaway that the family frequented. It sold sports equipment and gramophones. The shop was owned by Prafulla Mahalanobis, the younger brother of Prasanta Mahalanobis, who was a renowned statistician and scientist and a close friend of Sukumar Ray. Satyajit Ray called him Bula Kaka. Now, Bula Kaka had a special chair in his shop that was also a weighing machine. Whenever the family passed by his shop, they made it a point to go inside, sit on the special chair and get themselves weighed.

A Hot Ice Cream

How do you like your ice cream—hot or cold? Isn't ice cream supposed to be cold, you might immediately ask. Not according to young Ray. As a child, Satyajit Ray had a weakness for ice cream. One day, Bula Kaka and his wife took him to see the port in Calcutta. The child was excited to see boats and ships of different colours and sizes anchored at the shipyard. On their way back, they stopped at a restaurant. When the ice cream was served, Satyajit couldn't wait to taste it. But after having just the first spoonful of ice cream, his teeth started aching. The child suddenly left his seat, ran to the waiter who had served them ice cream, and whispered something to him. Whatever he had said amused the waiter. He then came to the table and said that the child had requested him to heat up the ice cream!

17

An Ear for Music

One of Satyajit's early teachers was his aunt Madhuri, or Bulu Pishi to him. She later married Bula Kaka. She gave him his first lessons in English. She read out stories from an English book and then retold them to Manik in Bengali. Many years later, his aunt once recalled in an interview that whenever she thought of young Manik, she saw 'a quiet boy, sitting alone, hand on cheek, thinking—or drawing or listening to music'. Ray had an ear for music right from his childhood. Even as an infant, he had noticed that when one rolled a marble over the stone slabs of the floor of the house, the sound of the marble changed as it passed from one slab to the other.

Two Gramophones and a Radio

Bula Kaka also gifted little Manik two toy gramophones and kindled a lifelong passion for Western music in him. One of them was produced in the UK and was called Pigmyphone. The other was a German import called Kiddiphone. There were also forty tiny records—the size of doughnuts—that came along with these gramophones. These were of marches and waltzes. Manik came to love them as much as the Tagore songs that he heard so often from his mother. When the radio station opened in Calcutta, Bula Kaka gave Manik a radio called the crystal set. It was quite different from the radios that we see now. It came with a pair of headsets, so only one person could listen to it at a time.

19

A New Home

About three years after Sukumar Ray's death, the family's printing business went bankrupt and the house in which Satyajit Ray was born, on Garpar Road, was auctioned off with all its belongings. Suprabha Devi moved with Satyajit to her brother P.K. Das's house in Bhowanipore in south Calcutta. There were a couple of things in his uncle's home that left Manik completely awestruck. The first was the floor of the house. It was embedded with pieces of china—mostly white, but a few with patterns such as flowers and stars on them. Manik would stare at this unusual floor for hours and often wondered how many cups and saucers would have been broken to make this floor! The second thing was the balcony right outside his bedroom, which looked out on a buzzing street. He would spend hours looking at hawkers on the street selling a variety of wares.

Pastries Anyone?

The one hawker whose voice sent a wave of joy in Manik's little heart was that of a man who used to come twice a week with his big wooden box with the name Mrs Wood hand-painted on it. In his big box the man carried the yummiest pastries, cakes and patties made by Mrs Wood. Manik's eyes would light up with delight when he heard his aunt calling out to the man, for that meant that tea that evening was going to be a grand affair— with the most delicious baked goodies to bite into!

Manik would also wait eagerly to have roasted and spiced chickpeas from a hawker who came each evening. As dusk gathered outside the balcony, the hawker would turn up with a straw basket perched on a kind of a padded cap on his head, singing, '*Babu main laya hoon mazedaar chana-chur garam!*'

21

Escape by a Hairbreadth

Manik's maternal uncle had an Erskine Sedan in which he would sometimes take Manik for a drive to Maidan, a tree-lined open space near Victoria Memorial in Calcutta. In the evening, many Englishmen used to play golf in Maidan and one had to be really careful, for there were always golf balls flying around! On one occasion, when Manik was a little unmindful, a ball came vrooming in his direction. That ball would have hit young Manik had his uncle's driver Sudheer Babu not pulled him aside in the nick of time! The ball flew past his ear and hit the railing of the Victoria Memorial instead.

The Magic Show

Manik's uncle also took him to many carnivals, circuses and magic shows. While Manik greatly enjoyed the carnivals and circuses, he was most fascinated by the magic shows. Once, his uncle took him to Empire theatre to watch an Italian magician called Shefallo. The magician talked continuously to hold the attention of the audience while he performed his tricks. Manik later found out that this incessant talk that magicians engage in is called 'patter'. Shefallo was followed by a woman magician called Madame Palarmo. She, on the other hand, performed her tricks in absolute silence, which left Manik completely spellbound.

23

A Dhoti-clad Magician

After a few months, Manik watched a Bengali magician perform some magic tricks at a wedding party. The magician was clad in a simple shirt and dhoti and looked quite like an ordinary man, but his skills far surpassed those of Shefallo and Madame Palarmo. Even without all the fancy props and a proper stage, he performed his tricks with great dexterity. He spread several matchsticks on the mattress on which he was sitting. Then he opened the empty matchbox and called, 'Come on now, all of you, one by one!' The matchsticks rolled towards the matchbox one by one and slipped into it—following the magician's orders like obedient puppets!

Meeting the Magician

A few days later, Manik bumped into the same magician near his house. Since Manik was very interested in magic, he had already started thinking of this man as his guru or teacher. 'I would like to learn magic from you!' Manik told the magician. 'Of course, child,' said the magician and took out a pack of cards from his pocket at once. He taught him a simple trick and asked him to practise. The magician then left. Manik and the magician never met again—for in all the excitement of meeting the magician, Manik had forgotten to take his address! However, Manik bought a few books on magic and practised tricks in front of a mirror, perfecting quite a few of them!

25

Starting School

During his early years, Manik was homeschooled by his mother. When he was eight-and-a-half, he joined Ballygunge Government High School, where the medium of instruction was mainly Bengali. He joined what would be considered Class 5 today. As his entrance test, the class teacher gave him four arithmetic problems to solve while sitting in another room. When Manik came back with the answers, the teacher was taking a lesson in English. He looked at the sheet and nodded, which meant that all the answers were correct. As Manik was taking back the answer sheet from the teacher, a boy from the class shouted, 'What's your name?' 'Satyajit,' Manik answered. 'What's your pet name?' the boy asked again. Manik had no idea that it wasn't advisable to reveal one's nickname in school so he innocently told him what he was called at home. After that, none of his classmates ever called him Satyajit—it was used only by his teachers.

A Gifted Artist

Manik was very good at drawing right from his childhood. His art teacher in school was very fond of him. One day the teacher asked the class to draw something. After the students were done, he started marking the students' drawings. When he looked at Manik's drawing, he smiled and marked it '10 + F'. The other students bent over Manik's desk and wondered what the 'F' stood for. One of them went to the teacher and asked: 'Why +F, Sir? What does the "F" mean?' The teacher looked at the student gravely and answered, '10 + First, "F" stands for "first".'

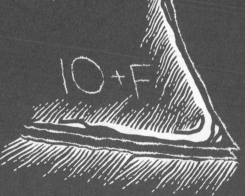

Gurudev's Autograph

When Ray was ten, his mother took him to Santiniketan to attend the Poush Mela, a festival held there annually in the winter. Ray had bought a new autograph book and wanted its first page signed by Rabindranath Tagore. He went to Tagore one morning and requested an autograph. Tagore asked him to leave the book with him and collect it the next morning. When Ray got his notebook back, along with the autograph there was a short poem in Bengali. Translated, it read:

For many a year, I have travelled many a mile
to lands far away
I've gone to see the mountains,
the oceans I've been to view.
But I failed to see that lay
Not two steps from my home.
On a sheaf of paddy grain—a glistening drop of dew.

The Tiger with a Burnt Tail

28

On another occasion, when Ray and his mother were visiting Santiniketan, he had carried a small drawing book. Sometimes he went to the Kala Bhavan, the fine arts centre in Santiniketan, to spend time with the famous artist Nandalal Bose. Once, Nandalal Bose drew a cow, a leopard, a bear and a tiger in Ray's drawing book. He finished drawing the tiger and put a small black patch at the tip of the tiger's tail. 'What's that patch for?' asked young Satyajit. 'Oh this!' said Nandalal Bose. 'You see, this tiger is very greedy. He walked into someone's kitchen to steal a piece of meat. That's when his tail caught in the hot stove and got burnt!'

Early Interest in Films

While still in school, Ray became a film fan, avidly following the lives of Hollywood stars like Hedda Hopper and Deanna Durbin (He wrote her a fan letter, to which he received a reply. He was not so lucky with Ginger Rogers and Billy Wilder.) in magazines like *Picturegoer* and *Photoplay*. He only watched Hollywood films then. He'd often watch films many times, sometimes just to learn the tunes of songs by award-winning American composers and lyricists Irving Berlin and Jerome Kern. Films featuring the popular dance duo Fred Astaire and Ginger Rogers were also among his favourites.

Love for Western Music

When Ray was thirteen, he once went looking for a bargain in music shops in Calcutta with one of his school friends. The treasures that he found hunting through the many shops were Beethoven's *Symphony No. 5* and Mozart's *Eine Kleine Nachtmusik* (*A Little Night Music*). After his great discovery, Ray lay awake the whole night listening to the records over and over again. The beauty of the classical Western music was not lost on Ray. He had read about Beethoven in one of the ten volumes of *Book of Knowledge* he had when he was younger, but now he was listening to his music completely enraptured. Over time, Ray developed a profound understanding of Western music. After hearing a symphony a couple of times, he could whistle the entire composition easily.

31

In His Father's Footsteps . . .

Ray passed the matriculate exam just before he turned fifteen years of age. On his mother's insistence, he joined Presidency College, where the medium of instruction was English, to study science for the first two years, but found that he disliked physics and chemistry. So, in his third year, following the advice of Prasanta Mahalanobis, who had been a friend of his father, he shifted to the economics course. Another reason for the change could be that an uncle had apparently promised him a job if he graduated in economics. He disliked that subject too, but graduated with a BA degree from the same college that his father and grandfather had. Ray completed his bachelor's degree at the age of eighteen.

A Student in Santiniketan

Ray wanted to try his hand at being a commercial artist straight after his graduation. However, his mother felt that he needed to learn art formally first. Ray was not keen to begin with, but in 1940 his mother persuaded him to study art at Santiniketan. Rabindranath Tagore had been a close friend of their family and his father had wished that his son would one day attend Tagore's institute. Ray enrolled as a student at Kala Bhavan, the art wing of Santiniketan. Trips to nearby villages for sketching exercises were the first encounters with rural life for the city-bred Ray. He was introduced to Oriental art—paintings of Ajanta and Ellora, Indian sculpture, miniature paintings, Japanese woodcuts and Chinese watercolours. Till then, his exposure to art had been limited to only the Western masters. But now, for the first time, he began to appreciate the unique qualities of Indian art.

Artistic Influences

One of the pioneering figures of modern Indian art and Ray's teacher at Kala Bhavan, Nandalal Bose, once told Ray: 'Draw a tree but not in the Western fashion. Not from the top downwards. A tree grows up, not down. The strokes must be from the base upwards . . .' This made Ray realize how art must also grow organically, just like life. Along with his three friends, he also undertook a tour of places of artistic interest in India. The tour drew his attention to the symbolism in Indian art, to the small details that signify bigger meanings—a quality that his films demonstrated greatly.

The Inner Eye

The eminent artist Benode Behari Mukherjee, who was also a teacher at Kala Bhavan, left a lasting impression on Ray. In spite of being severely myopic in one eye and blind in the other, Ray felt that Benode Behari Mukherjee was an extraordinary artist. Even when Benode Behari Mukherjee became completely blind a few years later due to a cataract operation gone wrong, he continued to create art. Ray was so inspired by Benode Behari and his art that many years later, in 1972, as a tribute to his teacher, he made a loving documentary on his life and works, titled *The Inner Eye*.

35

Music and Films in Santiniketan

Western classical music had been a passion for Ray since he was a child. He also loved watching films. Even during his time in Santiniketan, he found means to pursue his interest in music and films. He made friends with a German professor of English, Alex Aronson, who was also very fond of music and had a good collection of Western classical music records. Ray spent many evenings in his cottage, listening to music on his gramophone. Ray also found books on cinema in the university library such as Paul Rotha's *The Film till Now* and Raymond Spottiswoode's *A Grammar of the Film*. Though Ray had great interest in films, up until this point the thought of becoming a film-maker hadn't really occurred to him.

Letters to His Mother

During his years in Santiniketan, Ray kept his mother up to date with his life there through letters. She got regular news of his progress in art classes, with mentions of his teacher Nandalal Bose. Rabindranath Tagore and his nephew, the artist Abanindranath Tagore, got many mentions too. Ray assured his mother that he was having his meals on time and that the dhobi washed his clothes well. His concern is obvious from his reminders to his mother to take her medicines on time and queries about the availability of insulin injections. He missed Calcutta a lot. He asked his mother to send him newspaper clippings of Western music concert reviews. He even complained to her about missing out on cricket matches and film screenings.

Back to Calcutta

Ray really missed Calcutta while he was in remote Santiniketan. He felt out of touch with the outside world and its goings-on. He especially missed watching films. The nearest cinema from his hostel was a couple of miles away and only mythological films were screened there, in which he had absolutely no interest. Soon, he started making weekend trips to Calcutta. He visited flea markets and shops that sold books and gramophone records. Mahatma Gandhi had just launched the Quit India Movement against the British Empire. The war was at Calcutta's doorstep. In December 1942, Ray decided to return to Calcutta.

Ray, the Adman

After returning to Calcutta, Ray took a job at a British-run advertising agency, D.J. Keymer. He joined the agency as a junior visualizer. He spent thirteen years in this agency until he became a full-time film-maker. He rose to be recognized as a star in the advertising world and worked on many successful ad campaigns. Ray was fascinated by typography—both Bengali and English—and used innovative calligraphic elements and Indian motifs in many of the advertisements that he created. Playing around with fonts and distinctive calligraphy became his signature style. He also developed four typefaces: Daphnis, Holiday Script, Ray Roman and Ray Bizarre— the latter two  went on to win an international typography competition in 1971.

39

A Graphic Artist

One of Ray's colleagues at D.J. Keymer, Dilip Kumar Gupta (DK as he was called), started a publishing house called Signet Press. Having worked with Satyajit, Gupta knew his strengths well. He asked Ray if he would like to design the covers for the books that he was planning to publish. He promised to give Ray complete artistic freedom and so Ray agreed. Ray designed covers for many books which were published under the Signet imprint, including *Banalata Sen* by Jibanananda Das, *Man-Eaters of Kumaon* by Jim Corbett, *The Discovery of India* by Jawaharlal Nehru, among others. Around this time, Ray also worked on the illustrations of the children's version of *Pather Panchali*, a classic novel by Bibhutibhushan Bandyopadhyay that had originally been published in 1929. It left a lasting impression on the young movie buff and was to change his life forever.

Calcutta Film Society

Ray watched and studied world cinema seriously, taking shot-by-shot notes of what worked and what did not work for him in a particular film. He would also take up a story or a novel for which a film had been announced and write its screenplay. Once the film was released, he would compare his screenplay with the film. He, along with a few of his friends such as Harisadhan Dasgupta and Chidananda Dasgupta, established the Calcutta Film Society in 1947. The club organized special screenings of Hollywood, European and Russian films—the very first film being *Battleship Potemkin* (1925), the silent film directed by Sergei Eisenstein. Soon, Ray began writing articles on cinema in magazines and newspapers too.

Meeting Renoir

In 1949, the famous French director Jean Renoir arrived in Calcutta to scout for locations and actors for his film *The River*. Renoir was the son of Pierre Renoir, the great Impressionist painter. His film *La Grande Illusion* (1937) was the first foreign-language film to be nominated for a Best Film Oscar. Ray came across a classified advertisement in the newspaper that Renoir was staying at the Great Eastern Hotel and would be interviewing actors for his new film. He rushed to the hotel, met Renoir and introduced himself as one of his admirers. Ray accompanied Renoir on two trips to locations outside Calcutta. Four decades later, receiving the Legion of Honour from the then French president François Mitterrand, Ray told him that he considered Renoir to be his 'principal mentor'.

Bicycle Thieves

In 1950, Satyajit's employers sent him to London for a five-month stint at their headquarters. He was married by then, and his wife Bijoya Ray shared his love for Western music and Hollywood films. The couple would sometimes skip meals so that they could watch the best films being screened at that time. But the one film that made a deep impact on Ray's mind was the Italian film *Bicycle Thieves*, directed by Vittorio De Sica. The film resonated with Ray on many levels and confirmed his belief in realistic cinema. It proved pivotal in helping Ray make up his mind to take a plunge into film-making.

43

The First Film That Wasn't

The first Bengali novel that Ray had wanted to make a film on was actually Rabindranath Tagore's *Ghare Baire*, many years before he started working on *Pather Panchali*. He even wrote the screenplay for it. However, negotiations with producers did not materialize and the project was abandoned. Years later, on reading his old script, Ray found it too melodramatic. He did, however, finally make *Ghare Baire* four decades later in 1984.

Song of the Road

Inspired by *Bicycle Thieves*, Ray decided to make his first film based on Bibhutibhushan Bandyopadhyay's novel *Pather Panchali*—the children's version of which he'd illustrated six years earlier. On his voyage back from London, he wrote the first draft of the screenplay. He also created a series of illustrations as the visual blueprint of the film. He would take his sketches to potential producers and explain the sequences. He was able to pique the interest of the producers but his idea of making a realistic film with on-site shooting found no takers. Undeterred, he put together a motley crew of technicians and a cast of mostly amateur actors. He started looking for locations and decided to shoot a few sequences of the film so he could prove his mettle to the producers.

Here One Day, Gone Another

The story of how *Pather Panchali* got made is nothing short of a film script by itself. To begin with, Ray had to borrow money against his insurance policy to start filming. He even sold some of his art books and records to supplement the funds. On 27 October 1952, he set out to take the first shot. It was the famous scene in the film where Apu and Durga see a train for the first time across the undulating field of kaash flowers. The shoot went off well and the crew decided to return the following Sunday to continue shooting the sequence since Ray was still in a full-time job at D.J. Keymer. The following Sunday when they returned, they discovered to their utter horror that all the kaash flowers had been eaten up by a herd of cows! They had to wait for the next season of flowers to finish shooting this sequence.

At Long Last

In early 1953, Ray found a producer who provided some funds, with a promise to release more if his own upcoming film did well. Ray took a month off from work and the unit started shooting. The film was shaping up well but the funding was running precariously low. Sadly, the producer's film was a dud at the box office and he was unable to provide more money. Ray's wife, Bijoya, pawned her jewellery and the shooting continued for a few more days. But work on the film came to a standstill after that. Ray continued approaching producers with some edited footage of the film. After many leads turned out to be dead ends, his mother finally came to his rescue. She requested a friend who knew the then chief minister of West Bengal, Dr B.C. Roy, to enquire if the government could help with funds. A meeting between Ray and the chief minister of was subsequently arranged. And finally, the government agreed to finance the film, allowing Ray to realize his vision.

47

If Not for Dr B.C. Roy . . .

Ray's mother Suprabha Devi had not been in favour of Ray quitting his secure job with a regular income to become a full-time film-maker at first—an understandable stance given their financial instability before Ray took up his advertising job. Interestingly, after Dr B.C. Roy was agreeable to a grant for Ray to complete *Pather Panchali*, some government officials who saw the footage did not understand the content of the film and mistook it for a documentary on rural upliftment. So, they put the loan down in their records as one given for 'road improvement', a probable association with the translation of the film's title, *Song of the Road*. Dr Roy extended his good offices even further—he arranged a special screening in Calcutta for then Prime Minister Jawaharlal Nehru, who was impressed enough by the film to recommend it as India's entry for the 1956 Cannes Film Festival in spite of reservations from different fronts. The film won the award for the Best Human Document at Cannes, one of many awards it won nationally and internationally.

The Harbinger of Good News

Days before Satyajit Ray received good news from the government about funding his first film, *Pather Panchali*, a white owl came and perched itself on the sill of his bedroom window. The owl, in Hindu mythology, is considered the vahana or vehicle of Lakshmi, the goddess of wealth. Many people in the neighbouring houses tried to lure it away by offering food. But the owl didn't budge, not one bit. It sat at the same spot for three consecutive days. In her autobiography *Manik and I*, Bijoya Ray writes: 'No one knew where she had come from, or where she went.'

Filming Resumes

After almost a year of interruption, the shooting of *Pather Panchali* resumed with the grant from the West Bengal government. But the money from the government came in instalments. Because of the many financial hurdles, the film was in production for nearly three years. In fact, Ray described three miraculous occurrences while making the film (referring to the characters in the film): 'One, Apu's voice did not break. Two, Durga did not grow up. Three, Indir Thakrun did not die.' Most of the music for the film was composed by Pandit Ravi Shankar. Given the prior commitments he had, Panditji was able to spare only two days and was only able to see about half the film. In an eleven-hour-long session, he recorded most of the music. The film's cinematographer, Subrata Mitra, who too played the sitar, provided additional music for the remaining score.

A Roaring Success

In 1954, Monroe Wheeler, a director of Museum of Modern Art (MOMA), New York, was in Calcutta. Purely by chance, Ray met Wheeler and showed him some stills of *Pather Panchali*. Wheeler liked the stills very much and offered to hold the premiere of the film at MOMA. And so he did—on 3 May 1955. Later that same year, it released in Calcutta. Initially, the film received a lukewarm response, but in a few weeks' time, everything changed. It struck the right chord with the audiences. The film went on to win eleven international awards, including the Best Human Document award at the Cannes Film Festival in 1956. Directed by a self-taught film director, shot by a novice cinematographer, embellished by a first-time art director, with a cast of amateur actors and on a shoestring budget, the film established India firmly on the world cinema map.

BEST HUMAN DOCUMENT AWARD

51

The Unvanquished

After the resounding success of *Pather Panchali*, the idea of doing a sequel to the film started taking shape in Ray's mind. Since Bibhutibhushan Bandyopadhyay's novel had a sequel, it lent itself naturally to a follow-up film that explored Apu's life through his adolescent years and his relationship with his widowed mother. Released a year after *Pather Panchali*, *Aparajito* is nothing short of a marvel. A landmark in the history of cinematography, the film's cinematographer Subrata Mitra invented the technique of 'bounce lighting' for the film by stretching layers of white cloth on the ceiling and training the lights on them—thereby achieving a unique quality of reflected light for indoor shots. The film also marked the beginning of Ray's use of ambient sounds to highlight the mood of the scenes. Though *Aparajito* was not a popular success, it was very well received critically. A timeless classic, it's a worthy successor to *Pather Panchali*.

The World of Apu

Pandit Jawaharlal Nehru, after watching *Aparajito* at a special screening, had famously asked Ray, 'What happens to Apu now?' Ray replied that he did not have a third film in mind. *Aparajito* had not been very successful at the box office, so Ray wrote the screenplay of his third film, *Jalsaghar*, based on a short story by Tarashankar Bandyopadhyay and made the fantasy comedy *Parash Pathar*. Just before the release of the film, he was invited to the Venice Film Festival to screen *Aparajito*. The film won the Golden Lion at the festival and garnered much acclaim. At a press conference during the festival, Ray was asked if he had a trilogy in mind and Ray heard himself say yes. *Apur Sansar*, the third and last film in the Apu trilogy, released in 1959, and went on to become both a critical and a box office success.

53

Back to School

Ten years after Satyajit Ray had finished school, he once went back for a reunion. When he entered the main hall of the school, he was amazed. What he had remembered as a huge hall now looked fairly small—and his head almost touched the top of the door! Not just the hall, even the playground, classrooms and benches appeared smaller to him. It took him a while to figure out why it was so. When he had left school, he was five feet three inches. And now, almost ten years later, he was six feet five. The school had, of course, not shrunk but he had grown.

Ravi and Ray

Satyajit Ray and Pandit Ravi Shankar were great friends. Shankar gave music to four of Ray's films—*Pather Panchali*, *Aparajito*, *Apur Sansar* and *Parash Pathar*. When Ray had approached Pandit Ravi Shankar to compose music for his first film, *Pather Panchali*, the latter gladly agreed. Pandit Ravi Shankar was so moved by the rushes of the film that he composed the music in four-and-a-half hours straight. Around this time, Ray had also conceptualized a documentary film on the legendary sitarist, which was to be shot during one of his recitals. Ray had even worked out a detailed storyboard for the film containing over a hundred detailed sketches and notes on the camera movements. He had tentatively titled it *A Sitar Recital by Ravi Shankar*. But for reasons unknown, the film didn't take shape and his plan to make a film on his musician friend remained a wish unfulfilled.

55

Famous *Khekor Khatas*

Ray preferred to sketch and write, rather than just write his scripts down. And, for that, he found that the traditional large, blank notebooks with the distinctive red cloth covers were ideal. He'd use about two such *khekor khatas* per feature film, filling them with musical notes, sketches for costumes, dialogues, set designs, details of scene-by-scene sequences and even film scripts in various stages of development, including the final shooting scripts, detailing of each scene and shot. He'd use these notebooks to draw out random sketches, diagrams and designs too.

Revival of *Sandesh*

In 1961, with the help of poet Subhash Mukhopadhyay, Satyajit decided to revive *Sandesh*, the Bengali children's monthly magazine his grandfather had launched in 1913. This decision willy-nilly made him a writer of science fiction, detective stories and supernatural tales for the monthly, besides designing the covers and doing most of the illustrations. He also handled the puzzles section. He was joined by his aunt, award-winning children's author Lila Majumdar (her father was Ray's grandfather's younger brother), and his cousin Nalini Das, whose home served as the magazine's office. Das wrote popular adventure stories featuring four girls, collectively known as Gandalu. *Sandesh* encouraged young readers to write and had a special section that carried their writings.

57 Films on Tagore Stories

Rabindranath Tagore was a profound influence on Satyajit Ray. He made as many as five films based on the short stories, novellas and novels written by Tagore—these include *Teen Kanya* (1961), a three-part anthology film (*Postmaster*, *Monihara* and *Samapti*) that depicts three female protagonists, their lives, aspirations and thoughts; *Charulata* (1964) and *Ghare Baire* (1984). In 1961, on the occasion of the birth centenary of Tagore, Ray also made a documentary on the life and philosophy of the great poet. Later, in one of his biographies, Ray referred to the documentary saying, 'Ten or twelve minutes of it are among the most moving and powerful things that I have produced.'

Charulata, Ray's Masterpiece

In 1964, Ray adapted Tagore's novella *Nastanirh* (The Broken Nest) into celluloid and named it *Charulata* (The Lonely Wife). Set in the late-nineteenth century, the film explores a woman's yearnings and her innermost conflicts. A marvellous example of visual storytelling, the masterfully nuanced film is considered one of the best adaptations of literature to cinema. Ray, apart from directing the film, also wrote its screenplay and remodelled a lot of elements from the original text by Tagore. Ray described the film as the one which has the least defects. In an interview with a magazine, when asked about his most satisfying film, Ray said, 'Well, the one film that I would make the same way, if I had to do it again, is *Charulata*.'

59

Places as Characters

Taking a page from Vittorio De Sica's book—one of his favourite directors—Ray preferred to shoot at actual locations, so that they could 'be a living backdrop to the film'. He preferred using available light too. *Pather Panchali* was shot on location, through different seasons in Boral, a small town in West Bengal, fitting the fictional village of Nischindipur perfectly. A few local residents were used in various roles, adding to the authentic look of the film. In *Kanchenjunga*, in which a family spends an afternoon in Darjeeling, Ray used shades of light and mist around the famous mountain to reflect the tension in this family drama. As such, the mountain is a character. For *Jalsaghar*, Nimtita Rajbari in Nimtita village, ten kilometres from Murshidabad, was perfect as Biswambhar Roy's palace, with his illusions of grandeur. In *Aranyer Din Ratri*, Ray makes the forest itself the protagonist of the story.

First Film in Colour

Kanchenjunga (1962) was Satyajit's first film in colour and his first film from an original screenplay, which he wrote in just ten days. The narrative follows Rai Bahadur Indranath Roy Chaudhuri, a successful and arrogant man, who has brought his large extended family to Darjeeling for a short holiday. In the course of the afternoon before they are to return to Calcutta, various family tensions are exposed in the seemingly happy group.

Ray used the play of sunlight, clouds and mist on the majestic Himalayas, to show the dynamics between the family of eight and the other players of this drama. The elusive, snow-covered mountain peak is finally visible only at the very end of the film, in bright sunlight.

61

Women in Ray's Films

The women characters in Ray's films have invariably stood out, leaving vivid impressions on their audiences worldwide. From Sarbajaya, Durga and Indir Thakrun in *Pather Panchali* to Charu in *Charulata*, from Dayamoyee in *Devi* to Arti in *Mahanagar*, from Bimala in *Ghare Baire* to Aparna in *Nayak*, from Duli in *Aranyer Din Ratri* to Jhuria in *Sadgati*, the women characters that populated the cinematic world of Ray had their own journey of trials and tribulations. Ray never shied away from depicting strong and independent women who were not confined to domesticity but often fiercely expressed their emotions, desires and conflicts. Ray defied unidimensional depiction of women and their complex identities were revealed through layers of the films' narratives. He broke away from the stereotypical roles that existed for women in Indian film for many years, giving us wonderfully real female characters who flouted labels and were way ahead of their times.

The Secret Superstars

One of Ray's most compelling cinematic representations emerge in his portrayal of his child characters, who appeared in almost all his films. Be it Apu and Durga in *Pather Panchali*, Kajol in *Apur Sansar*, Ratan in *Postmaster*, Mrinmoyee in *Samapti*, Mukul in *Sonar Kella* or Pikoo in *Pikoor Diary*, each child character in Ray's films transcends the boundaries of celluloid and steps into the hearts of viewers—to remain there forever. Ray had a rare insight into a child's mind, a knack of looking through a child's eye. He had even devised his own way of directing children. Uma Dasgupta, the actor who played Durga in *Pather Panchali*, once recalled that Ray never gave instructions to the children in the presence of others. It was always whispered exclusively to each child so that what he wanted them to do was like a secret between just the child and him.

63

Ray's Documentaries

Though Satyajit is famous the world over for his feature films, there are five documentaries that are an integral part of his diverse portfolio. The first, *Rabindranath Tagore* in English, was released in the birth centenary year (1961) of Tagore, who was born on 7 May 1861. The next, *Sikkim* (1971), again in English, showcased its music, dance, art, handicrafts, people and stunning countryside. *The Inner Eye* (1972), a documentary in Bengali on Benode Behari Mukherjee, covers his life and art from his childhood till his blindness. It was awarded the Best Information Film (documentary) at the twentieth National Film Awards. *Bala* (1976) is a documentary in English on a Bharatanatyam dancer, Balasaraswati. Ray's last documentary, made in Bengali, and commemorating the birth centenary of his father, was *Sukumar Ray* (1987) who was born on 30 October 1887.

Two, A Film Fable

Two (1964), a twelve-minute silent film, has Satyajit doffing his hat to a genre he admired. It was part of a trilogy of short films from India, commissioned by the US Public Television under the banner of 'Esso World Theater', a cultural programme telecast by PBS (Public Broadcast Service) and sponsored by the American oil company ESSO. The profoundly allegorical tale about two young boys, one poor and one rich, explores complex subjects such as socio-economic divide, loneliness, consumerism and contentment through the almost palpable competition between the two boys over their toys. The rich boy's bedroom window is what figuratively separates the two boys and their distinctly different lives. Finally, when the poor boy's free-flying paper kite is shot down by the rich boy's air gun, he feels that he has won. But has he?

Ray's Homes

Satyajit was born at 100 A, Garpar Road. He moved with his mother when he was five to his maternal uncle's place at Bakul Bagan. The family moved to Beltala Road in 1932 and then to Rashbehari Avenue in 1934. Once Ray started working, he moved with his mother to a separate apartment in Ballygunge Gardens. After he married Bijoya, Ray moved from an apartment at No. 31 Lake Avenue to one at No. 3 Lake Temple Road which was his home from 1959 to 1970. This office-cum-home saw many landmarks of his life. He acquired his first piano here, after which he started composing the music for his films too. The Professor Shonku and Feluda series were written here. *Sandesh*, the magazine started by his grandfather, was revived here. And it was in this home that he lost his mother on 27 November 1960. And finally, there was 1/1 Bishop Lefroy Road (1970–1992), his final home—the one that Ray's admirers visit in Kolkata even today.

Ray the Foodie

Ray was quite a foodie. He loved dining out. He used to visit the famous Flurys in Calcutta every Sunday morning for breakfast. He preferred mutton over chicken and, while he relished continental cuisine, he thoroughly enjoyed the Bengali fare. He especially loved luchi, arhar dal and begun bhaja. He also loved to eat muri, or puffed rice, mixed with ghee and sugar. Ray was very particular about his eating habits and his regular food in the studio was usually chicken sandwich and curd. In his cult classic, the fantasy-adventure-comedy-musical *Goopy Gyne Bagha Byne*, the legendary film-maker went all out with his love affair with food as the king of ghosts bestows Goopy and Bagha with three boons—the first of them being that they could get unlimited delicious food just by clapping their hands!

67

The Tale of Two Simpletons

Ray's most favourite story, written by his grandfather, was the humorous fantasy *Goopy Gyne Bagha Byne* (The Adventures of Goopy and Bagha)—a story of two tone-deaf musicians who nurse aspirations of making it big and are helped by a kind, boon-giving king of ghosts. The story first appeared in 1915 (six years before Ray was born) in *Sandesh*. Ray decided to make a fun-filled adventure fantasy film for children based on the story. But the producers baulked at the idea of making a film for children on an extravagant budget. After several attempts, Ray did finally find a backer, though he had to scale down the project significantly. He had planned to do the entire film in colour but had to be content with filming only the closing sequence in colour. The film turned out to be one of the greatest box office hits in the history of Bengali cinema and ran non-stop for close to a year in some theatres in Calcutta.

GGBB in Hindi

Not many know that after the success of his fantasy-adventure film *Goopy Gyne Bagha Byne*, Ray had wanted to remake the film in Hindi. The legendary poet, lyricist and film-maker Gulzar started work on the script for the film. But when he was halfway through the script, Ray had to shelve the film, probably because of a rift with the producers. Fifty years after the release of Satyajit Ray's *GGBB* in 1969, an animated adaptation of the classic, directed by Shilpa Ranade, was released. It is based on the Hindi translation of the original by Gulzar.

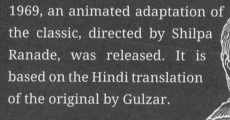

The Magic Slippers

If you've watched *Goopy Gyne Bagha Byne*, you would probably remember the scene where Goopy and Bagha are both rolling in the snow. To shoot this scene, the cast and crew of the film went to Kufri in Shimla. When the camera was ready, the two actors, Tapen Chatterjee and Rabi Ghosh, started rolling down the hill covered with snow. Once the shot was over, the actors scrambled to their feet and announced, 'We've lost our slippers!' These were the magic slippers that the king of ghosts gives to Goopy and Bagha as a boon. They were made specially for the film and had big ghost eyes painted on them. For the next half an hour, the crew dug through the thick blanket of snow to look for the slippers. But they were nowhere to be found. The crew, however, was quite amused to think of the possible reaction of the locals if they found slippers with ghost eyes painted on them during the summer months when the snow melted away!

Ray the Lyricist

Ray's multi-genre musical masterpiece *Goopy Gyne Bagha Byne* was originally written as a four-page story by Upendrakishore Ray Chowdhury. So, Ray had to tweak it to introduce drama and songs. Made on a shoestring budget, the film saw Ray donning multiple hats—director, screenplay writer, music composer, lyricist, dialogue writer and even as a playback singer. The film has ten songs, which were all written by Ray and immortalized by his multilayered lyrics, mellifluous melody and awe-inspiring picturization. Ray even lent his voice to one of the songs in the film—*Bhuter Rajar Bor Deoa.*

71

Classical Indian Musicians

While Satyajit's love and knowledge of Western classical music is well-known, he worked with many Hindustani classical musicians for his films, starting with sitar player Pandit Ravi Shankar who composed the scores for the Apu trilogy and *Parash Pathar*. In *The Inner Eye*, a sitar composition by Pandit Nikhil Ranjan Banerjee plays evocatively in the background. The music for Ray's ode to Hindustani classical music, *Jalsaghar* (1958), was by sitar player Vilayat Khan. Sitar and surbahar exponents Imrat Khan and Wahid Khan featured too, as did shehnai maestro Ustad Bismillah Khan. Begum Akthar sang and played the part of Durga Bai, a singer. Sarod player Ustad Ali Akbar Khan composed the music for *Devi*.

The Music of Ray

Ray always believed that music was one of the most intrinsic elements in establishing the sensibilities of a film. For most of his early career, Ray worked with the musical maestros of Hindustani classical music, relying on their understanding when it came to composing music for his films. Soon he realized that though these maestros were unmatchable musicians, he had his own vision for the music in his films. So, he decided not to rely on any other composer and started composing music for his films. *Teen Kanya*, based on three short stories by Tagore, saw the birth of Ray the music director. He started work on the music right from the script stage of the film—he created a particular theme for each of his films, which formed the background score. He could play the piano with professional ease and could be found on most evenings in front of his Roland piano, trying out tunes for his films and writing musical notations with a fountain pen.

The Calcutta Trilogy

Satyajit's take on the turbulent Bengal of those times is portrayed in this trilogy. *Pratidwandi* (1970), based on the novel by Sunil Gangopadhyay, is about the struggles of a middle-class man (starring Dhritiman Chaterji in his film debut) during the Naxalite movement in Bengal, who cannot relate to his activist brother or his ambitious sister. *Seemabaddha* (1971), based on a novel by Sankar, portrays the dark side of corporate life, filled with ambition and greed. And *Jana Aranya* (1976), also based on a Sankar novel, is the story of a young protagonist's fall from innocence while he tries to make a living. Ray uses a song by Tagore as a haunting background, highlighting the young man's dilemma about the compromise he chooses, or has to make.

The Socio-Political Influence

Ray's views on politics and society were reflected in his films, whether it was the heady power of unquestioning faith in *Devi* or emancipation of women in *Mahanagar*. In *Hirak Rajar Deshe*, Satyajit brings up the powerlessness of the oppressed and the importance of education. In *Ashani Sanket*, Ray examines the effect of the great Bengal famine of 1943. In *Ganashatru*, Ray shows how blind faith and rampant corruption make a well-meaning, concerned doctor an enemy in the eyes of his patients. *Ghare Baire* has a nationalist battling the British through the Swadeshi movement, after the partition of Bengal (1905), and a wife torn between tradition and love. In his last few films, his disappointment over eroding morals and his anger with the prevailing corruption became more evident.

75

Ghare Baire, Finally

Ghare Baire (1984), based on a 1916 novel by Rabindranath Tagore, was the first film that Ray had wanted to direct. The story is set in 1907, focusing on three main characters—the beautiful Bimala, wife of the aristocratic, genteel and wealthy Nikhilesh, and his diametrically opposite friend, the charming, fiery Sandip who arrives as a guest. In the chaos following Lord Curzon's partition of Bengal, which brought about massive agitations against it by Indians, the Swadeshi movement to boycott British goods became a rallying call. Sandip, a champion for the cause, is eloquent and convincing in his point of view. His impassioned rants against British rule and his seductive ways strike a chord in Bimala's heart, as her husband watches on helplessly, as does the audience. Bimala is caught between the two. At the 32nd National Film Awards, it won the award for Best Feature Film in Bengali.

Films Other Than His Own

Ray donned many hats. He was not only a prolific director, but also a music composer, calligrapher, fiction writer, set designer, graphic designer and a film critic. Apart from working on his own films, he contributed to many other films too. He wrote the screenplay and composed the music for the Bengali film *Baksa Badal* (1970) directed by Nityananda Datta. Ray had written the screenplay for the Hindi film *Target* (1995) and the Bengali film *Uttoran* (1994), both directed by Sandip Ray. Some of the English documentaries for which Ray had done the screenplays are *Our Children Will Know Each Other Better*, *The Brave Do Not Die* and *Creative Artists of India: Satyajit Ray*. The first two were directed by Harisadhan Dasgupta and the third by B.D. Garga. He composed the music for two Merchant Ivory Productions films *The Householder* (1963) and *Shakespeare Wallah* (1965). In addition, he also edited *The Householder*.

77

Literary Pursuits

Ray's multifaceted personality is quite obvious from his films—which he not only scripted and directed, but for which he also made costumes, designed posters, created beautiful sets and composed music. But one of the most endearing aspects of Satyajit Ray was his fiction writing, primarily for teenagers and young adults. His own youthful fantasies influenced the themes in his stories aplenty. From detective fiction, sci-fi and ghost stories to magic, fantasy and even time-travel adventures, Ray's fascinating stories are evidence of his perceptive yet extremely playful mind. The lucid language, fluid storylines, abundant details and thorough character portrayals in his literature make it popular with readers across ages and generations. He also created two of the most enduring characters in Bengali children's literature—Feluda the astute sleuth and Professor Shonku the illustrious inventor.

The Dozen Stories

Ray, as a child, was fascinated by science, magic, ghosts, crime fiction and the supernatural. This fascination comes through in the collection of short stories he published in bunches of twelve. The names of these anthologies were a play on the Bengali word for twelve, *baro*, or dozen, *dajon—Ek Dajon Gappo* (One Dozen Stories), *Aro Ek Dajon* (Another Dozen), *Aro Baro* (Another Twelve), *Ebaro Baro* (Twelve Again), *Eker Pithe Dui* (Two upon One) and *Bah! Baro* (Wonderful Twelve). Ray also designed the covers of the anthologies, with a distinct play of typography. Funny, intriguing and utterly imaginative, the stories in the dozen series bear the signature of Ray's extremely visual style of writing and masterful storytelling.

Feluda Mysteries

Satyajit Ray had read all of Sherlock Holmes in his school days. Inspired by his childhood love for Sherlock Holmes, he wrote the first draft of a short story that featured a young boy, Topshe, and his cousin Prodosh C. Mitter, also known as Feluda, who possessed unbelievable analytical and detective abilities. Ray once explained the wordplay on the protagonist's name: '"Pro" stands for "professional", and "dosh" is the Bengali word for "crime". The "C" is "to see", that is, "to investigate". So, it works out as Prodosh C. = Professional Crime Investigator!' The first story of Feluda's exploits—*Feludar Goendagiri* (Danger in Darjeeling)—was published in *Sandesh* in 1965. Ray wrote a total of thirty-five published Feluda stories and four unpublished ones, all narrated in first person by Topshe. These spine-tingling suspense stories, apart from offering chills and thrills, also introduce readers to numerous places and a host of interesting trivia. Perhaps this is why Feluda remains one of the most popular detectives Bengali literature has ever seen!

Feluda on Celluloid

Ray made two Feluda films. The first one was made in 1974, based on his novel *Sonar Kella* (The Golden Fortress) and introduced the charming young detective and his teenage assistant to the world. An epic adventure like no other, the story takes Feluda all the way to Jaisalmer to save a young boy who claims to remember facts from his past life. Ray made the second Feluda film, *Joy Baba Felunath* (The Mystery of the Elephant God), in 1979, in which Feluda meets his arch-enemy Maganlal Meghraj. In both these films, Soumitra Chatterjee breathed life into Feluda. After the death of Santosh Dutta, who played Jatayu, one of the main characters in the Feluda stories, Ray decided to never make a Feluda film again, although he went on write Feluda stories till the end of his days. Subsequently though, many Feluda films and telefilms have been made and many actors have portrayed the charismatic Feluda.

81

The Sci-Fi-Loving Genius

Even though Ray was not formally trained in science, he had a scientific temperament and was deeply interested in science. As a child, he loved reading the works of H.G. Wells and Jules Verne and was fascinated by aliens, artificial intelligence, space travel, parallel universes and robots. Through a number of stories, Ray explored the genre of science fiction from multiple angles—and one of his best-known creations is the middle-aged, balding, unassuming but ingenious inventor, Professor Shonku. In the 1960s, Ray wrote the script of a fascinating sci-fi adventure film called *The Alien*—which was loosely based on his story *Bonkubabur Bandhu*, published in *Sandesh* in 1962. Unfortunately, the project never took flight. Ray was also the president of the one-of-a-kind Sci-Fi Cine Club set up in 1966 in Calcutta by science fiction enthusiasts. All the design-related work for the club—right from the logo to invitations to brochures—was done by Ray himself. The club was active for about three years.

Professor Shonku Stories

Professor Shonku (Trilokeshwar Shonku) was a fictitious character created by Ray, who is said to have found inspiration in an Arthur Conan Doyle creation, Professor Challenger, and in Hesoram Hushiar, a character created by his father, Sukumar Ray. The first story *Byomjatrir Diary*, about space travel, appeared in *Sandesh* in 1965. In all, Ray wrote thirty-eight science fiction stories led by the eccentric and brilliant Professor Shonku, the last one being *Swarnaparnee*, about a visit by Shonku to Germany, just before World War II, which appeared in the special Puja issue of *Anandamela*, a children's bi-monthly magazine in 1992. Incidentally, Ray had designed the first cover of this magazine in March 1975. Professor Shonku's servant Prahlad and his cat Newton feature in many of the stories. The last Professor Shonku story, titled *Intelectron*, was not completed.

83

Professor Shonku's Inventions

Among the many characters created by Ray, none is as loved as the scientist-inventor Professor Shonku. He had his own laboratory in his house in Giridih where he invented offbeat, low-budget gadgets, a few of which can be seen in the first screen adaptation of a Professor Shonku story. Some of his magical inventions include Miracurall, a drug that cures all ailments except the common cold (the name is the short form of Miracle Cure for All Ailments); Annihilin, a pistol capable of annihilating any living species; Shonkoplane, a small hovercraft based on anti-gravity technology; Omniscope, which is a combination of telescope, microscope and the X-ray-scope; Air-conditioning pill to keep the body temperature normal in extreme climate as well as Fishpill which is space food for cats.

Professor Shonku O El Dorado

Professor Shonku O El Dorado (Professor Shonku and El Dorado) is a film directed by Sandip Ray. It is based on *Nakur Babu O El Dorado*, a story by Satyajit Ray of Nokur Chandra Biswas/Nokur Babu, who has the power to see the future. Nokur Babu visits Professor Shonku and warns him about São Paulo in Brazil, where Professor Shonku has been invited to attend a scientific conference. Dhritiman Chaterji, who acted in three films—*Pratidwandi*, *Ganashatru* and *Agantuk*—directed by Satyajit and two directed by Sandip Ray, portrayed Professor Trilokeshwar Shonku. For many, the roller-coaster ride from India to Brazil, the Amazon forests, the mythical El Dorado and Los Angeles with Professor Shonku was a nostalgic trip back to their childhoods. The film in Bengali and English was released on 20 December 2019 as a Christmas release.

Ray the Translator

Apart from being a writer and editor, Ray was also a skilled translator. After the publication of Sukumar Ray's *Abol Tabol*, nobody dared to translate it into English for the longest time as it was considered impenetrable to the English readers in its very literary play. But, in 1970, Ray himself rose to the challenge and brought out a limited-run translation of his father's book. His preoccupation with the language and logic of nonsense literature, and perfect sense of rhyme and rhythm, make it an exquisite translation. Ray also translated other books of nonsense literature from English into Bangla, including *Toray Bandha Ghorar Dim*, a collection of limericks and nonsense rhymes by Lewis Carroll, Edward Lear and Hilaire Belloc.

More Writings for Children

Ray always believed that children have a far more fertile imagination than older readers, and hence, wrote primarily for younger audiences. Apart from his engrossing suspense stories of Feluda and the utterly imaginative stories of the fictitious scientist Professor Shonku, he created a number of other works for children. One of the most incredibly gripping of these is *Fotikchand*, a dramatic mystery novel that he wrote about the botched kidnapping of a young boy. The book was made into a film in 1983 by his son Sandip Ray. Satyajit Ray is considered a great writer of horror stories as well, having spun more than twenty of them. There are also his endearing Tarini Khuro tales. Satyajit Ray even collected stories of Mulla Nasiruddin and translated them into Bangla as *Molla Nasiruddiner Galpo*, or Tales of Mulla Nasiruddin.

Bijoya, Ray's Better Half

Bijoya Ray was born on 27 October 1917, as the youngest of four daughters. She grew up in Patna. As she had a good voice, her father had wanted to send her to Paris to be trained but he passed away in 1931, when she was only thirteen. So, the family moved to Calcutta to her paternal uncle Prasant Das's house. This is where Monku (Bijoya) first met Manik. She graduated from Jogamaya Devi College, after which she taught at Bethune Collegiate School and Kamala Girls' School, Calcutta. She then moved to a job in the government. She quit that job to go to Bombay to start a film career. She acted and sang a playback song in a Bengali feature film called *Shesh Raksha* (1944) and acted in *Mashaal* (1950) too. She didn't face the camera after that, except for *Gaach* (1998), Catherine Berge's documentary on Soumitra Chatterjee. After she married Ray, their only son Sandip was born in 1953.

Behind the Scenes

Bijoya was a constant source of inspiration and influence in Ray's life. She was the first to read every screenplay, every story he wrote, starting with the storyboard and notes of *Pather Panchali*—Ray wrote most of it on their journey back from England by ship. She also managed the costumes for his films. Bijoya and Ray would often go together to buy props, from antique furniture to sari borders. She held the film unit together—ensuring that everyone was fed and arrived on time. She was like a mother figure to the young actors on Ray's sets. Her favourite actor was Uttam Kumar and was quite thrilled when Ray cast him in *Nayak*. Her one indulgence was perfume, which she used without fail, picking some up from every country she travelled to with Ray. After Ray's death in 1992, she lived in Calcutta with her son Sandip, daughter-in-law Lalita and grandson Saurodip. Her autobiography, *Amader Kotha*, was first published by Ananda Publishers. She died on 2 June 2015, aged 97.

Ray's Only Hindi Telefilm

Sadgati (1981), an adaptation of a short story by Munshi Premchand, was produced by Doordarshan. The fifty-two-minute film focused on the evils of the Indian caste system through the insurmountable predicament of Dukhiya, a poor and low-caste Chamar (whose traditional profession is tanning leather), and his wife Jhuria, in the hands of the Brahmin priest by whom the date of his daughter's marriage needs to be fixed. The Brahmin demands free labour that Dukhiya, played by Om Puri, cannot refuse as he has no choice. Unwell, weak and hungry, Dukhiya goes about the strenuous chores with a sense of hopeless resignation, felt by the audience with every blow he aims at the block of wood he is trying desperately to chop with his feeble blows, only to collapse forever.

The Historian's Craft

For his first Hindi feature film, Satyajit chose historical fiction—*Shatranj Ke Khilari* (1977), based on a short story by Munshi Premchand. Set in 1856, just before the British annexed the princely state of Awadh, the story is about two nobles, Mirza Sajjad Ali and Mir Roshan Ali, who are focused only on the game of chess, quite oblivious to the chaotic state of their kingdom. Ray was a tireless and outstanding researcher— he studied in great detail every possible resource, from books about chess and reproductions of Company School paintings to numerous travelogues, so as to get the ambience, food, clothing, mannerisms and music of the period in which the story is set absolutely right. In keeping with the authenticity of those times, an appropriate mix of Urdu, Hindi and English is used in the film too.

91

Ray's Banned Film

Sikkim is a documentary film made by Ray. It was commissioned by Palden Thondup Namgyal, the twelfth and last Chogyal (king) of the Kingdom of Sikkim in 1971, at a time when Sikkim was still an independent country. When Sikkim merged with India in 1975, the film was banned by the Government of India since the film was about the sovereignty of Sikkim. The ban was finally lifted by the Ministry of External Affairs (MEA) in September 2010. In November 2010, at the 16th Kolkata Film Festival, the documentary was screened for the very first time for the public, who had gathered in large numbers to watch a Ray film. However, before any more screenings could be held, the director of the film festival received an injunction from the Sikkim High Court, banning the film yet again.

Of Symbols and Metaphors

Once, Ray was screening *Mahanagar* in a European film festival. After the movie ended, a film critic came up to Ray and told him how deeply impressed he was with the symbolism that he'd used in the final scene, which ends in two street lamps—one lit and the other unlit—in the foreground and the jobless couple (Anil Chatterjee and Madhabi Mukherjee) merging with the city's teeming millions. The critic showered praises on Ray for showing the street lamps to display the contradicting emotions of hope and hopelessness of the jobless couple. Ray simply said that it wasn't intended to mean anything. It was typical of Calcutta for the streetlights not to be working properly and though it makes the shot more interesting because it adds another layer of meaning to it, it was a mere coincidence.

93

Photographer Extraordinaire

Glamour of the Gods: Hollywood Portraits was the title of an exhibition held from 7 July–23 October in 2011 at the National Portrait Gallery in London. It included seventy portraits, mainly black-and-white, of legendary Hollywood actors and actresses, from the collection of John Kobal, a film historian. A photograph of John Kobal and John Russell Taylor (an art and cinema critic and biographer) taken by Satyajit Ray in Delhi in 1969 was inexplicably included among the otherwise familiar subjects like Elizabeth Taylor, Ingrid Bergman, Vivien Leigh, Cary Grant, Fred Astaire and James Dean. Kobal had liked film festivals and attended one in Delhi in 1969 when John Russell Taylor and Ray were on the festival's jury. Kobal suddenly decided that the other three jury members (Russian Alexander Zharki, Argentine Leopoldo Torre Nilsson and Satyajit), who were film-makers, should photograph him and Taylor, and because he had found Ray's photograph quite remarkable, it was included in the exhibition.

Three Greats at the Taj

94

After the Delhi Film Festival in January 1977, Ray, Akira Kurosawa, the Japanese director, and Michelangelo Antonioni, the Italian film-maker left early enough with a few others for Agra to see the Taj Mahal in the first light of dawn. Three of cinema's great masters of their time chatted informally as they walked around the monument. In the course of their chat, Ray spoke about a huge tree in India that measured almost one mile in girth. Much later, Kurosawa wrote to him, reminding him of that incident, 'I have always felt from the first time I met you that you are the kind of man who is like a huge tree. A great tree in the woods in India.'

Praise from Other Directors

Directors from around the world have held Ray in very high esteem. To quote but a few:

'Not to have seen the cinema of Ray means existing in the world without seeing the sun or the moon.' — Akira Kurosawa

'I'm also a big fan of Satyajit Ray's body of work. The few interactions I had with Ray are memories I treasure.' — Martin Scorsese

'We know of Indian cinema through Ray's works and, to me, his best is Devi, *a cinematic milestone.'* — Francis Ford Coppola

'I have had the pleasure of watching Mr Ray's Pather Panchali *recently, which I hadn't seen before. I think it is one of the best films ever made. It is an extraordinary piece of work.'* — Christopher Nolan

'In Ray, I have noticed a complete filmmaker. He has mastered the art of scriptwriting, direction, editing and scoring music—which very few in the world can equal. If he were in Hollywood, he would have proved a tough challenge for all of us.' — Elia Kazan

Ray's Favourite Actor

Soumitra Chatterjee (19 January 1935–15 November 2020) was best known internationally for his collaborations with Ray, with whom he worked in fourteen feature films and one documentary. It was said that some of Ray's screenplays were written with him in mind. He was also a stage actor, director, playwright, author and poet. Though his roles as Apu in *Apur Sansar* and Amal in *Charulata* made him world-famous, his role as Feluda made him a cult figure at home. When Soumitra asked Ray to suggest a name for a magazine he had founded with Nirmalya Acharya in 1961, Ray suggested *Ekkhon* (Now) and designed the inaugural cover page. Soumitra was awarded France's highest civilian award—the Chevalier of Legion of Honour—in 2017, thirty years after his mentor Ray was awarded.

A Documentary About His Father

Sukumar Ray (1987), the thirty-minute Bengali documentary, was Satyajit's tribute to his brilliant father, who had achieved so much in the short span of his life. It was narrated by Soumitra Chatterjee, who also played a small role in the film. It covers some of Sukumar's drawings for his children's books, his formation of the Nonsense Group in college, his handwritten humorous magazine *Thirty-two and a Half Fries*, his collection of poems *Abol Tabol*, his novella *HaJaBaRaLa*, his short story collection *Pagla Dashu* and his play *Chalachitta Chanchari*. The documentary also focuses on the family lineage, Sukumar's college days in London while studying photography and lithography, his meeting with Rabindranath Tagore, his association with the Brahmo Samaj and the publication of his first poem *Khichuri* in the children's magazine, *Sandesh*. Satyajit went back to 100 A, Garpar Road, the only home he revisited, while filming this documentary.

Carrying On His Legacy

Sandip Ray—Satyajit Ray and Bijoya Ray's only child—was born on 8 September 1953. He is a film director, composer, scriptwriter and producer. He had started helping his father on many of his sets much earlier, but his career formally took off at the age of twenty-two as assistant director of *Shatranj Ke Khilari*. *Fotikchand* (1983), the first film Sandip Ray directed, based on Satyajit Ray's story, won an award in the International Children's Film Festival in Vancouver. He also directed and composed the music for seven feature films on the Feluda stories authored by his father. *Professor Shonku O El Dorado* (2019), the first film on Professor Shonku, played by Dhritiman Chaterji, was directed by him. In 2012, Sandip introduced audiences to yet another popular character created by his father, Tarini Khuro, in *Jekhane Bhooter Bhoy*. Some of Sandip's other well-known films are *Nishijapon*, *Hitlist*, *Chaar* and *Monchora*.

Rare Honours

Ray won many awards, national and international, starting with his very first film *Pather Panchali* (1955) and that was just the beginning. It won Best Film at the 3rd National Film Awards (1955), 7th Berlin International Film Festival (1957), 1st San Francisco International Film Festival (1957) and the Prix du document humain prize at the 9th Cannes Film Festival (1956). He won the National Award for Best Director six times. Ray received the Dadasaheb Phalke Award (1984), the Légion d'honneur (Legion of Honour) in 1987 and the Bharat Ratna (1992). He was also awarded an honorary doctorate from the Royal College of Art (1974), a Doctor of Letters from the University of Oxford (1978), the British Film Institute Fellowship (1983) and two Sangeet Natak Akademi awards (1959, 1986). Satyajit Ray received an Honorary Academy Award in 1992, becoming the first Indian to receive one. He received the Award for Lifetime Achievement, capping a career unsurpassed by any.

The Last Hurrah

When Ray was informed that he would be receiving an Honorary Award from the Academy of Motion Picture Arts and Sciences, it is said that he requested that his favourite Hollywood actress, Audrey Hepburn, present it to him. And so she did. For the 64th Academy Awards on 30 March 1992, from the Dorothy Chandler Pavilion in the Los Angeles Music Center, USA, Hepburn presented his award virtually. Ray accepted the award on tape from his hospital bed in Calcutta, which was beamed via video link to the audience at the Oscar ceremony, along with his acceptance speech.

Ironically, both Ray and Hepburn were dying. He passed away a few weeks later on 23 April 1992 and she passed away a few months later, on 20 January 1993, of cancer.

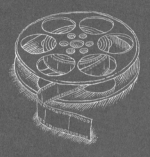

TRIVIA AND MORE

Satyajit Ray's Family Tree

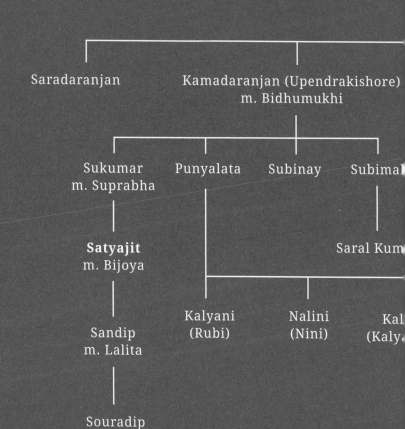

Saradaranjan

Kamadaranjan (Upendrakishore)
m. Bidhumukhi

Sukumar
m. Suprabha

Punyalata

Subinay

Subimal

Satyajit
m. Bijoya

Saral Kum

Sandip
m. Lalita

Kalyani
(Rubi)

Nalini
(Nini)

Kal
(Kaly

Souradip

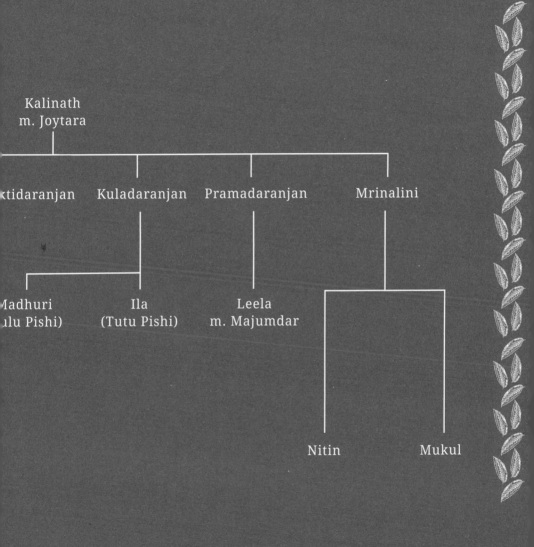

Kalinath
m. Joytara

ktidaranjan   Kuladaranjan   Pramadaranjan   Mrinalini

Madhuri   Ila   Leela
ulu Pishi)   (Tutu Pishi)   m. Majumdar

Nitin   Mukul

Satyajit Ray Filmography

1955   *Pather Panchali* (Song of the Road)

1956   *Aparajito* (The Unvanquished)

1958   *Parash Pathar* (The Philosopher's Stone)

1958   *Jalsaghar* (The Music Room)

1959   *Apur Sansar* (The World of Apu)

1960   *Devi* (The Goddess)

1961   *Teen Kanya* (Three Daughters)

       The Postmaster

       Monihara

       Samapti

1962   *Kanchenjunga*

1962   *Abhijan* (The Expedition)

1963 *Mahanagar* (The Big City)

1964 *Charulata* (The Lonely Wife)

1965 *Kapurush-O-Mahapurush* (The Coward and the Holy Man)

1966 *Nayak* (The Hero)

1967 *Chiriyakhana* (The Zoo)

1968 *Goopy Gyne Bagha Byne* (The Adventures of Goopy and Bagha)

1969 *Aranyer Din Ratri* (Days and Nights in the Forest)

1970 *Pratidwandi* (The Adversary)

1971 *Seemabaddha* (Company Limited)

1973 *Ashani Sanket* (Distant Thunder)

1974 *Sonar Kella* (The Golden Fortress)

1975 *Jana Aranya* (The Middleman)

1977 *Shatranj Ke Khilari* (The Chess Players)

1978 *Joy Baba Felunath* (The Elephant God)

1980 *Hirak Rajar Deshe* (Kingdom of Diamonds)

1981 *Sadgati* (The Deliverance)

1984 *Ghare Baire* (The Home and the World)

1989 *Ganashatru* (Enemy of the People)

1990 *Shakha Proshakha* (Branches of the Tree)

1991 *Agantuk* (The Stranger)

Documentaries

1961 *Rabindranath Tagore*

1971 *Sikkim*

1972 *The Inner Eye*

1976 *Bala*

1987 *Sukumar Ray*

Special Mention

1964 *Two*

1980 *Pikoor Diary* (Pikoo's Diary)

Satyajit Ray Film and Television Institute

Satyajit Ray Film and Television Institute (SRFTI) is an autonomous academic institution of cinema education. It was set up in Kolkata in 1995, by the Government of India, under the Ministry of Information and Broadcasting. The first session began on 1 September 1996. Named after the legendary film maestro, the aim of the institution is to train and bring to the fore creative and innovative film and television professionals in the country. Presently, the institute conducts a three-year postgraduate programme in cinema in six specializations of film-making; and a two-year postgraduate programme in electronics and digital media. The institute also conducts short courses on film appreciation, acting, digital editing and so on.

Selected Bibliography

- Robinson, Andrew. *The Inner Eye*. Andre Deutsch Ltd London, 1989.
- Ray, Satyajit. *Childhood Days: A Memoir*. Penguin Random House India, 1998.
- Ray, Satyajit. *My Years with Apu*. Penguin Random House India; New Edition, 2000.
- Ray, Satyajit. *Our Films, Their Films*. Orient Blackswan, 2001.
- Seton, Marie. *Portrait of a Director*. Penguin Random House India, 2003.
- Ray, Satyajit. *Speaking of Films*. Penguin Random House India, 2005
- Ghosh, Nemai. *Manik Da: Memories of Satyajit Ray*. HarperCollins India, 2011.
- Ray, Bijoya. *Manik and I: My Life with Satyajit Ray*. Penguin Random House India, 2012.